IBOGAINE EXPLAINED

PETER FRANK & ERIC TAUB

Copyright © 2012 Peter Frank

All rights reserved.

ISBN-13: 978-1484087374
ISBN-10: 1484087372
LCCN: 2013907679

DEDICATION

This book is dedicated to all the amazing people who have made ibogaine treatments possible. Because of your hard work, thousands of lives have been saved.

CONTENTS

1	Introduction	Pg 1
2	Origins	Pg 6
3	History in the West	Pg 14
4	Addiction Interruption	Pg 22
5	Spiritual, Emotional, and Physical Healing	Pg 38
6	The Science	Pg 46
7	The Law	Pg 53
8	Three Current Issues	Pg 60
9	Is Ibogaine Right for Me?	Pg 64
	Notes	Pg 67
	Medical Disclaimer	Pg 70
	Contact Authors	Pg 71

CHAPTER ONE
INTRODUCTION

I decided to write this book while visiting an ibogaine treatment center in Costa Rica. While there, I met a wonderful American man who had three kids, went to church every week, and loved camping and hunting. He had also been an addict for 15 years. He came for an ibogaine session out of desperation. His tolerance to methadone had skyrocketed in the previous six months. He needed three doses per day to prevent withdrawals, and his health and personal life were deteriorating. He did not know if ibogaine would work, but he had no other choice.

His ibogaine experience went exceptionally well. For the first three days, he felt terrible as the ibogaine brought up many of the emotional traumas that had led to his addiction. But on the fourth morning he had a huge smile on his face. He told us that he had absolutely no cravings, his emotions were stable, and his body felt great. He had called his wife in the US and she told him that he sounded like his 16-year old self, before his addiction began.

Later on, he told me that he wished he had taken ibogaine much earlier. If he had, it would have saved him and his family a lot of pain and money. He had known about ibogaine for a long time, but had delayed treatment because he could not find reliable information about it. Right then, I felt that I had to write a book for people like him—people who need a clear, unbiased source of information about ibogaine. This book is the product of that desire.

Who This Book Is For

I have made two assumptions about the reader of this book. First, that you know absolutely nothing about ibogaine. Second, that you are interested in an ibogaine session for yourself or for someone you are close to.

I have written this book as simply and clearly as possible. I only present the essential information, so as not to overwhelm you with pointless details. I only give you information that I know is true. To guarantee that my information is correct, I cross checked my facts with several other experts. In cases where I am not totally sure about an issue, or where there is debate among experts, I have indicated the limits of my knowledge. Although each chapter covers a discrete topic, I recommend that you read the chapters in the order presented.

This book is geared towards a person who is interested in an addiction interruption session. I cover ibogaine's history and introduction to the West. I walk the reader through a typical session, I discuss some complications, and I talk a lot about what to do after taking ibogaine. I also summarize the scientific findings on ibogaine because they are informative about its ability to help with drug addiction. Finally, I talk about ibogaine's legal status around the world.

I recommend reading "Chapter 4: Addiction Interruption" more than once. It contains more information than you can retain in a single reading.

This book is also useful for people who are interested in a psycho-spiritual session. It will give you all the background information that you need. It will not, however, tell you what an ibogaine session is like. I have found that everyone's experience is different, and so reading about other people's experiences is not very helpful. If you are interested in hearing first-person accounts of ibogaine sessions, there are plenty of videos and testimonials on the internet.

Basic Facts About Ibogaine

Ibogaine is a natural extract from the iboga bush, which is native to West-Central Africa. According to experienced users of psychedelics, it is the most powerful psychedelic in the world. Everyone who has taken ibogaine reports that the session is the most intense experience of their life. At the same time, however, ibogaine is gentle. It will not overwhelm you like LSD or other synthetics. People do not have panic attacks or psychotic breaks while on ibogaine. In fact, no one has ever reported being hurt by an ibogaine session. The worst case scenario is that you spend the entire time fearfully resisting your thoughts and waiting for the ibogaine wash out of your body.

A basic ibogaine session will last for two days. For the first 12 hours, you stay alone in bed. On the outside, you appear to just be lying there, but you are actually going deep inside your own mind. Some people have visual experiences, others just think a lot. For the next 12 hours, you will slowly come down from the peak intensity. 24 hours after initially taking ibogaine, you can walk around, eat, and talk; but you will be extremely sensitive. Many people report feeling like a new-born baby during this phase. Over the next day, your ego will slowly pull itself back together until you are ready to function in the world. Although it is possible to return to normal life after two days, most people want at least a week of rest before dealing with challenges of ordinary life.

Ibogaine is best known in the West for its use in "addiction interruption." It is especially effective for opiates and alcohol, but it also works for crack/cocaine, methamphetamines, nicotine, and any other drug. When addicts take ibogaine, they can get clean without experiencing withdrawal symptoms. Some never experience cravings again, but most people's cravings eventually return in a weaker form after several months. If people use these their months of freedom to change their lives, then they can resist the cravings when they return and stay clean for good.

Many people also take ibogaine for psychological and spiritual growth. It can take a person deep into their psyche and help them cope with unconscious issues. It can also make a person feel more connected to the universal Being that pervades everything. Today more and more people are recognizing that psychedelics like ibogaine are an excellent addition to psychotherapy, meditation, and contemplation.

Ibogaine has a miraculous quality about it, for both addiction interruption and psycho-spiritual purposes. Many people say that it totally transformed their lives. But it is far from a magic bullet. The crucial element is always the person's intentions. If they wish to be free from suffering, ibogaine can help. But if they still want to run from their internal pain, then ibogaine can do nothing more than bring short-term relief.

CHAPTER TWO
ORIGINS

Ibogaine is a single compound extracted from the root of the *Tabernanthe iboga* bush, which contains several other less potent psychedelic compounds. The iboga bush is native to West Central Africa and is used by practitioners of the Bwiti religion in Gabon.

The origins of iboga are lost to history, but there are plenty of myths. In one, nomads possessing unusual intelligence and joy introduced iboga to the settled tribes of Western Africa hundreds of years ago. The legend claims that these nomads appeared from the Congo jungle, taught the settled tribes how to eat iboga, and vanished back into the jungle, never to be heard from again.

In another legend, a young hunter discovered iboga through the intervention of a magical spirit. The young man, who was the most skilled hunter in his village, had been chasing a wild boar for many days. The boar led him into a part of the jungle that no man had ever entered. After silently approaching the boar after many hours, the hunter got close enough to throw his spear. He threw with all this strength, but just as the spear was about to kill his prey, the boar vanished in a whiff of smoke. When the hunter went to retrieve his spear, he found it stuck in the root of a bush. He dug up the root, ate it, and went into a deep trance. In this trance, the boar appeared to him as the spirit of the jungle and transformed him into the first iboga shaman.

In my favorite myth, iboga comes from the African Rift Valley, where the human race originated. In this story, early humans ate iboga as part of their natural diet. The iboga acted as a catalyst for their consciousness and caused them to develop language, a notion of time, and a sense of self. As they migrated out of the Rift Valley, they retained a faint memory of iboga that reappeared as the story of Adam, Eve, and the Tree of Knowledge.

A lot more is known about iboga's history in Gabon over the last century. In the 1920s, ritual use of iboga increased sharply in Gabon as the dominant tribe in the country, the Fang, began incorporating the Bwiti religion of the Matsongo, a much smaller tribe. According to Matsongo legend, they had learned how to eat iboga from pygmies in the forest.

Many Fang were attracted to Bwiti in the 1920s because their traditional way of life was confronting powerful new challenges. The global influenza epidemic of 1918 had reached the Fang villages and killed a large proportion of the population. A missionary reported that the flu claimed the lives of a quarter of the people in one village. At the same time, the spread of venereal disease caused rising infertility, a psychologically devastating condition for a culture centered on the family.

Contact with Europeans also had a strong effect. French merchants set up lumber camps that attracted a lot of young men from the villages. As a result, local agricultural output plummeted, and a famine occurred in 1924. The attraction of jobs and other opportunities caused a migration to the coast, depopulating inland villages. Finally, the overwhelming dominance of the Europeans in all aspects of life shocked the Fang and caused them to question their place in the universe. To cope with the shock, many Gabonese adopted Christianity and began imitating Europeans.

Bwiti represented an alternative path, one that blended traditional animism and ancestor worship with Christianity. Bwiti allowed its practitioners to exist in a changing world but protected them from completely losing their identity. Bwiti also offered a belief system that transcended tribes and could form the basis of a new Gabonese identity.

Between the 1920s and 1960s, the popularity of

Bwiti fluctuated. At its peak in the 1920s, around 20 percent of the Fang tribe practiced a form of Bwiti. This number dropped during the 1930s and 1940s but rose again after decolonization. In general, the degree of government repression has determined the popularity of Bwiti.

During the French colonial era, both the Catholic missionaries and the anti-clerical bureaucrats opposed Bwiti, albeit for different reasons. Catholic authorities considered Bwiti a form of pagan idolatry, and they spread rumors that Bwiti practices included human sacrifice and cannibalism. The administrators of the French colonial system opposed Bwiti mainly because its practitioners could not be induced to work for the modernization of the country.

Ironically, the postcolonial government of Gabon has had a similar position. Although Bwiti was officially recognized and protected by the government, Gabonese Christians were suspicious of the religion. In several instances, Gabonese Christians violently attacked Bwiti churches and practitioners. Meanwhile, the secular Gabonese elite, who wanted to see their country integrated in the world economy, had little patience for a religion they viewed as archaic and superstitious.

Bwiti is a difficult religion to characterize, because it lacks centralization, hierarchy, written teachings, and other structures of organized religion. Each Bwiti church is effectively autonomous, although many churches associate with a "mother church" and follow its practices. Different Bwiti churches emphasize different themes. Some focus on ancestor worship, others on animism and healing, and others incorporate a lot of Christian symbols and beliefs. Individuals are not bound to any particular church, so movement between churches is common.

I had a conversation with a Bwiti shaman that gives a good sense of how the religion blends different themes. He said that the iboga bush is a living spirit with its own intelligence and volition. If the iboga spirit approves of a person who has eaten the plant, the spirit will transport the person to the land of the dead. Once there, he meets with his ancestors, who are his guardians. He can ask his ancestors for advice or support; he can also ask his ancestors to request a favor from God (who I understood as the Christian God). According to the shaman, God rarely listens to people who are alive, because they are too far away. God is more likely to listen to the dead—therefore, if you want God to grant your request, you should get your ancestors to intercede on your behalf.

The Bwiti use iboga for two purposes. They take small doses at weekly ceremonies, and they take large quantities when facing a crisis. During the weekly ceremonies, practitioners eat a few spoonfuls of the root. This dose makes them energized and euphoric, but does not induce visions. These ceremonies last all night and involve singing, dancing, and listening to sermons given by the head of the church. Both men and women attend.

People who have participated in these rituals report feeling calm, content, and happy for days afterward. The Fang have a word, *engôngôl*, which roughly translates to "suffering." Bwiti practitioners believe that all humans live in a state of *engôngôl*, a philosophy that is reminiscent of Buddhism. They also believe that even though this suffering cannot be permanently overcome, the ritual use of iboga makes life more enjoyable.

Once or twice in a practitioner's life, he will ingest a large amount of iboga. The purpose of eating so much is to have the iboga "break open the head" and send the person's soul to the land of the dead. Once in the land of the dead, the person receives visions, instructions, and aid from ancestors and other spirits. People choose to embark on these vision quests for a variety of reasons: they are infertile or sick, their marriages keep falling apart, they would like to make more money, they are curious about the truth of life, etc. We can assume that these people are getting the answers they seek, given that the Bwiti religion has grown despite all the pressures working against it.

Those of us in the West can learn a few lessons from the Bwiti use of iboga. Bwiti teaches us that we should not romanticize pre-modern human societies. Bwiti is not a static, "traditional" African religion with centuries of history. Bwiti emerged over the last one hundred years as the people of Gabon were confronted with European colonization, Christianity, secularism, and capitalism - the same forces that shape the lives of us in the West. Just as the followers of Bwiti do not cling fearfully to some imagined past, neither should we.

Bwiti shows us that there is no single way to incorporate iboga into our lives. Different Bwiti churches have different practices that are based on their own history, circumstances, and preferences. Also, individual practitioners of Bwiti move between churches as their needs change. In the same way, Westerners will have to be creative in how they use iboga and other psychedelics. Different people will be attracted to different practices and rituals, and a person's needs will change over time. Instead of seeking a single path, we should find what works for us.

Finally, Bwiti offers us a warning about the limits of psychedelics. Practitioners of Bwiti, even those who regularly take iboga, still have the normal problems of life. Their relationships sometimes fall apart, their jobs can be unsatisfying, they get sick and die, and they experience the same existential emptiness that inflicts all humans. Iboga offers relief and can be of enormous help in times of crisis, but it does not save them from the basic dilemma of being alive. In the same way, psychedelics can doubtlessly offer a lot to Western civilization, but they cannot solve all our problems.

CHAPTER THREE
HISTORY IN THE WEST

Ibogaine's story in the West revolves largely around three individuals. Howard Lotsof discovered ibogaine by accident in 1962 and was an evangelist for the plant until his death in 2010. Eric Taub began quietly providing ibogaine to addicts and spiritual seekers in the mid-1990s. By the early 2000s, he was regularly training other providers. In one way or another, almost all ibogaine clinics in the world can be linked to Taub. Since 2005, Dimitri Mugianis has been the charismatic face of ibogaine. He has inspired newspaper articles, TV shows, and documentaries, and he is doubtlessly responsible for the public's growing awareness of ibogaine.

Howard Lostof was given a dose of ibogaine by a friend when he was nineteen years old and addicted to heroin. His friend, a chemist, did not know why his lab had ibogaine in storage; neither of them knew anything about the plant other than its hallucinatory properties. Lotsof had experimented with hard drugs for many years, and so taking a strange psychedelic seemed like a fun adventure to him. Later that night, he ate the ibogaine and had an intense, unpleasant trip where he experienced his own birth and relived many scenes from his childhood. Thirty-six hours later, he walked out of his apartment, resolved to never take ibogaine again. He looked up into the sky and realized that, for the first time in his life, he was not afraid. Even more surprisingly, he found that he was not craving heroin.

Thus began Lostof's lifelong involvement with ibogaine. During the 1960s, he facilitated ibogaine sessions for around twenty people in his social circle in New York City. Seven of them were opiate addicts, and five of them remained clean after their treatments. By their own admission, the other two were socially attached to using heroin and did not want to stop. His experiments ended in 1967 when the Food and Drug Administration (FDA) made ibogaine illegal.

In the 1980s, Lostof became heavily involved in advocacy and experimentation. He established a nonprofit organization committed to promoting ibogaine, the Dora Weiner Foundation. He also partnered with Dr. Charles Kaplan at Erasmus University in the Netherlands to conduct human trials. Beginning in 1989, they treated around forty heroin addicts before the death of a participant brought an end to the project (a subsequent investigation by Dutch authorities did not conclude that ibogaine was the cause of death). After the university ended the formal study, Lostof continued to work informally with Dutch heroin-user groups. He also funded some animal studies at Albany Medical School.

During the 1990s and 2000s, Lostof's activities were restricted to advocacy. He continued to raise awareness by writing articles, giving public talks, meeting with academics, and pressuring the FDA to make ibogaine available for research. He organized conferences around the world that helped knit the disparate ibogaine communities. Many people in the ibogaine world consider Lotsof to be the "grandfather" of the ibogaine movement. After his death in 2010, hundreds of people from all over the world gathered in New York to commemorate his legacy.

If Lostof was the public face of ibogaine, Eric Taub was the silent partner who quietly built an infrastructure of ibogaine providers across the Western Hemisphere. Taub heard about ibogaine in 1989 from a friend who had seen a public talk given by Lostof. After meeting Lostof and spending several years learning about ibogaine, he flew to Africa in 1992.

Taub planned to purchase thousands of doses of ibogaine, go to Zurich's Needle Park where addicts congregated, and treat thousands of people overnight. This plan turned out to be unrealistic.

Upon arriving in Cameroon, Gabon's northern neighbor, Taub could find only one chemist capable of extracting ibogaine from the iboga root. The process cost about $1,500 per dose and yielded small quantities. Taub bought thirteen doses and returned to the US.

He published an article in *Magical Blend*, a New Age magazine in San Francisco, and requests for ibogaine sessions came in quickly. For the next few years, Taub treated several people a month and flew back to Cameroon whenever his supply ran low. At this stage, he mostly provided ibogaine to people who wanted to have a spiritual experience, although he also treated a few addicts.

By the late 1990s, Taub's work with ibogaine intensified. He found a chemistry lab that could extract ibogaine for less than $150 per dose and produce it in large quantities, which eliminated his supply problems. The development of the Internet meant that more people, especially addicts, were learning about ibogaine's potential. Once Taub created a website, the number of people requesting a session increased dramatically.

Taub began training other providers, many of them former addicts. They spent time with him learning how to properly administer ibogaine, and he helped them set up practices of their own. Over the next decade, Taub helped establish practices in Brazil, the Netherlands, Costa Rica, Guatemala, Thailand, and several cities in Mexico. Many providers did underground treatments in the United States and Canada. Taub connected providers who he did not train with the chemists that he used, facilitating a global supply chain for ibogaine. More recently, he helped people open centers in Thailand, India, and Spain. By his own estimate, Taub has personally treated around 750 people, clinics working directly with him have treated another 1,400, and providers who he has supported have treated thousands more.

While Taub generally avoided publicity, Dimitri Mugianis had the limelight thrust upon him. A man of extraordinary charisma, wit, and personal integrity, Mugianis generated a lot of publicity for ibogaine over the last decade. Unlike Lostof and Taub, Mugianis came to ibogaine the hard way.

Born in Detroit to a family of Greek immigrants, Mugianis used drugs heavily in his teenage years. His drug use blended with his other passion, being a musician in the 1970s Detroit punk scene. By his early twenties, he had moved to New York City where he got involved in the avant-garde music culture, and his drug use escalated.

For his first few years in New York, he had a wonderful time. Drugs made him more creative in his music and more energetic on stage. He befriended many other musicians, many of whom were also drug users, and found a home in a community of addicts, activists, and artists. He also saw warning signs: friends overdosing, his relationships with non-addicts deteriorating, and the financial burden of an escalating habit. He tried to stop using several times but could not stay clean for long.

During the 1980s, Mugianis's drug habit had become increasingly destructive. He lost his musical creativity and his health fell apart. His community of friends collapsed, with people getting arrested, dying from overdoses, and being killed in drug deals. HIV appeared and hit his circle hard. He moved back and forth between New York and Detroit, trying to get clean and stay clean, but nothing worked.

He moved back into his parents' basement in Detroit and lived like a zombie for several years. He left the house only to raise money to cover his addiction to methadone, heroin, and crack. He had few friends and no life, and he began wishing for death. His only wish was to return to Greece, a place he had visited as a child. He felt that Greece was the land of his ancestors and that he should to go once more before dying.

Mugianis knew that he had to get clean before he could take this trip. Having heard about ibogaine while living in New York, he began searching for providers. He got in touch with Taub, who directed Mugianis to a clinic in Amsterdam. Mugianis had his treatment in May of 2002; it was physically and psychologically grueling, but he emerged from the session completely free of cravings.

Mugianis traveled to Greece and then returned home to Detroit. After a few months of resisting conventional treatments, he finally joined a twelve-step program, found a therapist, got a job, and began making art again. He gradually healed his past traumas and built a new identity. In the back of his mind, he began to feel a calling to treat other addicts with ibogaine. After two years of staying clean, he called Taub and asked to be trained as a provider.

Taub sent him to New York in 2005 to participate in an ambitious summer-long project. The goal was to treat as many methadone addicts and train as many providers as possible. Mugianis, along with several other people, participated in about fifty treatments. When the summer ended, he stayed in New York and began providing sessions for people all over the world. Since then, he has treated hundreds of addicts.

Mugianis has brought a lot of publicity to ibogaine. He is at the center of several documentaries, such as the film *I Am Dangerous with Love,* an episode of *Drugs, Inc.* on The National Geographic Channel, an episode of *Vice* on HBO, and a segment on *This American Life* on PBS. He regularly gives radio interviews, talks at conferences, notably the Harm Reduction Conference, and appears in public to advocate for ibogaine.

Aside from Lostof, Taub, and Mugianis, several other individuals have contributed to the ibogaine movement in notable ways. Claudio Naranjo, a psychologist known for popularizing the Enneagram, introduced ibogaine into San Francisco in the early 1960s. Since then, a few people have facilitated ibogaine sessions in the Bay Area but have not attempted to raise public awareness about ibogaine or create treatment centers elsewhere. Deborah Mash, PhD, a researcher at the University of Miami School of Medicine, has conducted over four hundred clinical trials, mostly in St. Kitts. Her hope is to develop a synthetic substance that treats addiction without causing hallucinations. Ken Alper, MD, a psychiatrist at New York University and a close friend of Lostof, has been ibogaine's main advocate in the medical community. He has published a number of academic papers on ibogaine and is researching 18-MC, a synthetic version of ibogaine.

CHAPTER FOUR
ADDICTION INTERRUPTION

Ibogaine does not cure addiction—people have developed the term "addiction interrupter" to describe its abilities. Ibogaine completely eliminates withdrawal symptoms from opiates. It also gets rid of cravings for opiates, cocaine, methamphetamine, and alcohol. Cravings are sometimes eliminated permanently, but it is more common for cravings to return after weeks or months, albeit in a weaker form. This means that ibogaine alone is usually not enough to kick a habit; people also need therapy and a change of lifestyle. In some cases, they must move to a new city and be in a whole new environment.

This chapter is broken into three sections. The first section walks through the four phases of an ibogaine experience. The first phase lasts about a day and a half. It involves entering into an altered state of consciousness and gradually returning to normal. The second phase lasts for another day and entails integrating the session. The third phase lasts about three months; during this time, people usually feel energetic, happy, and free of cravings. The fourth phase begins when emotional pain inevitably resurfaces and the person must confront it.

The second part of the chapter discusses complications with three specific drugs. The first is long-lasting opiates, which can cause withdrawal symptoms weeks after a session. The second is crack, cocaine, and meth, whose effects on the brain cannot be completely undone by ibogaine. The third is alcohol. Ibogaine cannot prevent heavy drinkers from going through "the shakes."

The third section summarizes a medical study that looked at all reported ibogaine-related deaths between 1990 and 2008. The paper could not conclude that ibogaine was the cause of death in a single case.

Four Phases of an Ibogaine Experience

The following is a description of a "typical" ibogaine session. Keep in mind that every ibogaine provider has their own protocols that may be slightly different from what is described here, but the broad strokes should be the same everywhere.

Phase One of your experience begins with your first dose and ends about a day and half later. You are given a tiny dose of ibogaine to test your reaction to it, usually when you begin experiencing withdrawal symptoms. If your reaction is fine, you are given a "flood dose." This large quantity of ibogaine eliminates your withdrawal symptoms and cravings. If you need more ibogaine along the way because you feel sick, you are given small doses called "boosters."

Ibogaine takes around one hour to kick in and another one or two hours to come on full force. Four hours after taking the flood dose, you are in an altered state of consciousness. It is impossible to describe the experience, and so I will not try. If you are interested, there are many accounts available online. People usually report two things that are worth pointing out. They say it is the most intense experience they have ever had, and they report having "visuals". Visuals are like movies that play in your head, even when your vision is normal. This is different from a hallucination, which alters your vision.

The visual aspect of an ibogaine session is often crucial to overcoming addiction. People often relive traumatic events from their past, particularly their childhood. They see how these traumas contribute to their current addiction, and they are often able to resolve the pain of the trauma. The visuals can be frightening, but they do not have to be. People often report a sense of peace and detachment even as they relive some of the scariest moments of their lives. The visuals are not essential; some people have no visuals and still benefit a great deal.

No one can predict what your experience will be like. You may have intense visuals, or you may simply have a lot of thoughts. You may be scared the entire time, you may feel calm and peaceful, or you may alternate between the two. You may feel nauseous and throw up, but your body may feel fine. My own experience with ibogaine is that the fear and discomfort are optional. If you remember that your thoughts cannot hurt you, there is no reason to be afraid.

Around ten hours after taking the flood dose, you will notice that your experience is getting less intense. The ibogaine is washing out of your system, you are more aware of your body, and you do not feel like your mind is strapped to a rocket ship. If you still feel withdrawal symptoms, your provider will give you boosters. These will not return you to the state of peak intensity; they just suppress the pain of withdrawal. As the next twelve hours go by, the intensity gradually wanes. Provided that you have not had a lot of boosters, you will be able to get out of bed and eat something around twenty-four hours after taking the flood dose. You may even sleep a bit.

You gradually transition into Phase Two. It is less intense than Phase One but challenging in its own way. You will be closer to your normal state of functioning. Your senses will work properly, you will be able to use your body, and you will feel more in control of your thoughts. But you will be exhausted at all levels. Your mind will feel like a dishtowel that is being wrung out, over and over. It will be difficult to focus on thoughts or maintain your concentration for very long. You may feel confused and disoriented. Emotionally, you will be on a roller coaster ride. You will feel like a sensitive newborn. You may cry a lot and experience waves of fear and sadness. You may also experience joy as you release repressed negative emotions.

The psychological issues brought up in Phase One may return for conscious processing. This can be challenging because your mind is too exhausted to run its normal repression mechanisms and so you cannot push the thoughts away. You will, at least to some extent, have to confront the contents of your mind. This can be painful, especially if you resist. On the plus side, you notice that your cravings are gone, perhaps for the first time in decades.

My own experience with ibogaine taught me not to resist Phase Two. If you accept your condition, Phase Two can be enjoyable. Your mind becomes so exhausted that it eventually goes almost completely still. Treat this as a nice vacation from the chattering mind. Calming the waves of repressed emotion is more difficult, particularly intense fear, but if you allow the emotions to fully wash through you, you will experience a blissful release that is priceless.

My advice is to calmly put your attention on the physical world. Go for a swim in the ocean, or sit in your backyard and notice how gorgeous the natural world is. Eat a piece of fruit; you will feel like you have never tasted anything so good. If you are really still, you can become aware of the one Beingness that pervades everything in the universe. In many ways, Phase Two is a precious gift in which you will feel intensely attuned to both the incredible beauty and the terrible pain of life.

Phase Three begins a day or two later and lasts for about three months. You enter this phase suddenly. In almost all cases, people fall asleep at the end of the Phase Two feeling terrible and wake up feeling fantastic. When you enter Phase Three, you are free of cravings, your mind is sharp, and your emotions are stable. You have a lot of physical energy, although this may take a while to come on. Many people are exhausted for a few weeks after their session, especially stimulant addicts.

Phase Three also has its challenges. This phase is temporary—it is not your new condition. You need to take the joy and energy that you received and use them to prepare for a new life. If you use this phase well, you will be able to resist your cravings when they return in Phase Four. If you squander this phase, you may end up right back where you started.

During this phase, you should contact a therapist; it is not necessary for the therapist to have experience counseling ex-addicts. More importantly, the therapist should be someone who you truly respect. Do not deliberately find someone you can manipulate or intimidate. The therapist should be the same gender as you. After years of doing treatments, many providers have found that addiction stems from unresolved emotional issues with the same-sex parent. A therapist of your gender will help you resolve these issues.

Consider joining a therapy group for ex-addicts. Some people have found Narcotics Anonymous to be useful, even when they disagree with its philosophies. If your entire social life has revolved around taking drugs, getting clean can be lonely and isolating. It is important that you connect with people who are going through the same challenges. You will need their support, encouragement, and companionship when hard times inevitably arise.

Do not return to your old scene, even if you are not experiencing cravings. People who do this invariably end up using again, because the social pressures are overwhelming. If you want to help your friends who are still addicted, tell them about ibogaine once and then leave them alone to make their own decisions. Spend a few years getting clean yourself, and perhaps you will then be in a position to help others.

In some cases, particularly if you were addicted to cocaine or methamphetamines, you should move to a new city. If you know how to reach a dealer in a few minutes, you may be overwhelmed by a craving after months of freedom. Being in a new location adds an extra layer between temptation and relapsing.

Find enjoyable ways to spend the time that you used to spend seeking drugs. Start practicing a sport that is fun for you: yoga, tai chi, and other martial arts are great ways to repair your body. Find a creative outlet that satisfies you such as music, painting, or poetry. It is also good to develop a spiritual practice. Now that you are not consumed by drugs, you will have a lot more time to wonder about the mysteries of life. This can be disorienting without some structure. Some people return to a traditional religion; others go to the New Age buffet. It is not particularly relevant what you choose. What matters is that you pick something that you will take seriously.

In the days after your session, make a treatment plan for yourself. Many providers will work with you and give you suggestions. If you spend the months of Phase Three building a life for yourself and getting a lot of support, your chances of staying clean permanently are pretty good. If you spend Phase Three hanging out with your old crowd and replaying old patterns, you will end up using again.

Phase Four can begin gradually or abruptly. You may notice that your old emotional triggers are slowly resurfacing, or you may find yourself screaming hysterically at your best friend or your children. Remember that ibogaine only gives your a vacation from your emotional pain for around three months; everyone eventually falls from the state of grace in Phase Three.

Keep in mind that emotional suffering underlies all addiction. Drug use is a way to numb you from pain, and repeated drug use leads to addiction and dependence. Even though emotional pain returns for everyone in Phase Four, it does not have to lead to cravings. And even if there are occasional cravings, these will not lead to addiction if they are not acted on.

For a few people, their cravings never return during Phase Four. These tend to be people who are older and have suffered a lot on drugs. They take therapy very seriously during Phase Three and deal with the issues that underlie their addiction.

Do not plan to be one of these people. You should expect to experience occasional mild cravings during Phase Four. Your old traumas will come up, and your first impulse may be to use drugs again. If you have not squandered Phase Three, you will be prepared when the cravings arise. If you truly desire to be free from addiction, you will find ways of managing your pain that do not involve drugs. Your therapy and your new life will provide you with ways to stay clean. Slowly, your pain will heal, and you will be permanently free of cravings.

Some people relapse. It may be that they did not plan adequately during Phase Three, or their addiction may have been unusually strong. They may have had a moment of weakness in which they used drugs, and that moment triggered a downward spiral. If you relapse, do not be too hard on yourself—just get back on your treatment program. Look into conventional therapies; many people find them more far more effective after an ibogaine experience. You can also consider another session. Some people do two or three ibogaine sessions before finally getting clean.

Age is a factor. People in their twenties and early thirties seem to relapse at a much higher rate. They feel that they are at the beginning of their lives and so they can spend a few more years as addicts. People in their late thirties and older usually stay clean, because they recognize that their time on this planet is finite and they do not want to waste any more of it.

I am indebted to Mugianis for making this final observation. This book implicitly talks about staying clean as a "success" and relapsing as a "failure." However, many of the people who relapse after an ibogaine session have an improved quality of life, even as addicts. They use less frequently and less intensely, they enjoy life more, and they have more hope because they know that it is possible to be free. So even if you relapse, you still may benefit a lot from your experience.

Complications with Three Classes of Drugs

Ibogaine is uniquely suited to helping people with opiate addictions. Ibogaine bonds with opiate receptors in the brain, eliminating withdrawal symptoms and cravings. The resolution of emotional trauma is helpful but not necessary. Even people who learn nothing during their session still come out free of cravings. Strangely, the length and intensity of a person's addiction is not a factor in the effectiveness of the treatment. People with twenty years of heroin addiction get the same benefit as a person who has spent a few years abusing painkillers.

Two opiates, however, present a challenge. Methadone and buprenorphine cause problems because they have such long half-lives. Methadone stays in the body for a few weeks, and buprenorphine stays in the body for months (the pills last for about two months, the film for three). This means that people start to experience withdrawal symptoms as the drugs wash out, regardless of whether or not they have done an ibogaine session.

In the early years of ibogaine treatments, many people with a strong methadone habit took ibogaine. They did not experience withdrawal symptoms during their session, and they came out completely free of cravings. When they went home, they and the provider thought that ibogaine had ended their addiction. A few days later, however, they began to experience mild withdrawal symptoms that persisted for a long time. Methadone addicts had a much higher rate of relapsing than addicts of other opiates. It took the ibogaine providers a while to realize what was happening.

By 2000, ibogaine providers became aware of this problem and developed a special treatment plan for methadone. This involved giving a lot of small doses early on, giving a flood dose, and following up with many boosters. This protocol eventually proved impractical, because it was so exhausting for the provider and the patient.

The newer protocol is to have people transfer onto a shorter-lasting opiate. For methadone, a person needs to be on shorter-lasting opiates for two to four weeks, depending on the severity of use. For buprenorphine, people need to be on a shorter opiate for several months. If this length of time sounds incredible, I assure you that many providers were shocked too. When buprenorphine became more popular in the early 2000s, providers treated it like methadone. But as buprenorphine users kept experiencing withdrawal symptoms, providers gradually increased the amount of time that people needed to be on shorter opiates. Providers eventually discovered that buprenorphine stayed in the body for several months.

Please do not let this dissuade you from moving onto methadone for a brief period. It is true that methadone is more addictive than heroin, its withdrawal symptoms are more severe, and it is worse for your body. But methadone allows you to think clearly and make long-term plans. It also gives you temporary freedom from the cycles of addiction. Many people have credited methadone with helping them get stable enough to plan an ibogaine session. Buprenorphine, on the other hand, is more difficult to recommend. It is more convenient than methadone, and its side effects are less severe, but it is also much more difficult to kick in the long run.

Crack, cocaine, and meth are the second class of drugs that are harder to treat with ibogaine. Long-term use of these drugs makes your brain insensitive to dopamine and serotonin, two neurotransmitters that make you feel happy. Ibogaine can temporarily alleviate cravings and repair some of the damage, but it cannot restore the brain to its natural state. Only time can do that.

Consequently, the treatment protocol for these drugs is longer and more intense than for opiates. Different providers have different plans, but the norm is to take two flood doses a week apart, with small boosters in the intervening days. These flood doses help repair some of the long-term damage and break the addiction, while the boosters prevent cravings from coming back. People tend to sleep through almost their entire treatment and often sleep eighteen hours a day in the weeks after their session.

It is crucial to move to a new city after treatment. Crack, cocaine, and meth users are far more likely to experience sudden, intense cravings in Phases Three and Four of their experience. If they know where to find drugs at a moment's notice, they will probably relapse.

These drugs create a strong addiction, but the situation is not hopeless. Many people have gotten clean using ibogaine, but they have taken the other aspects of treatment seriously. With opiates, it is possible for a person to take ibogaine, be lazy with other aspects of treatment, and still get clean. With crack, cocaine, and meth, ibogaine by itself will not be that effective. Moving cities, getting a good therapist, and situating oneself in a supportive social environment are absolutely essential.

The third drug that bears mention is alcohol. As with opiate addiction, ibogaine is incredibly effective for alcohol addiction. People long addicted to alcohol can get sober after a single flood dose; they rarely even need boosters. However, ibogaine cannot prevent "the shakes" that occur in people with extreme habits. Over the years, a few people have died during a session because of alcohol withdrawal. These people hid their alcohol addiction from their provider, went into withdrawal in the middle of a flood dose, and died from a seizure. Severe alcoholics need to go through "the shakes" before their session. Then, ibogaine can be an extremely effective tool.

Ibogaine-Related Deaths

A medical paper published in 2012 examined all known cases of ibogaine-related deaths between 1990 and 2008 outside of Gabon. The researchers found nineteen cases from around the world; fifteen of these cases involved opiate addiction interruption. In several cases, people were also addicted to cocaine and alcohol. The researchers had to rely on documents produced by local investigators. They admitted that this was not ideal because of the poor knowledge about ibogaine among police and medical examiners. The paper did not find conclusive evidence that ibogaine was the sole cause of death in a single case.

In nine cases, the cause of death was heart failure. For several years, ibogaine providers have known that ibogaine can exacerbate heart problems. People with a history of heart attacks or irregular heart rhythms are not good candidates for an ibogaine session. Today, almost all providers require an electrocardiogram (EKG) before giving a treatment. Fortunately, this problem affects only a small number of people.

In two cases, the cause of death was ibogaine's interaction with other drugs, notably opiates. It is not clear why, but if a person takes an opiate while on ibogaine, the effect is usually fatal. Over the years, a few people smuggled heroin into their ibogaine session and shot up in the middle of a flood. Please take this as a serious warning to not bring opiates with you to a session.

The cause of death for one person in the study was pancreatic failure. This person had been a heavy drinker, in addition to being an opiate addict, and had hepatitis. The cause of death for another person was an overdose; he self-administered the iboga and took far too much. In two other cases, the cause of death could not be determined.

Taken together, these cases indicate that there is a small risk to an ibogaine session. If you do not want to die, the best policy is to be completely honest with your provider and follow his instructions exactly. Your provider knows the risks and her job is to keep you safe; if you cooperate fully, then you will almost certainly be safe.

CHAPTER FIVE
SPIRITUAL, EMOTIONAL, AND PHYSICAL HEALING

Many people take ibogaine for purposes other than addiction interruption. People are often drawn to ibogaine and other psychedelics to accelerate their spiritual and psychological development. The timeline for one of these sessions is similar to the timeline for addiction interruption sessions, but the Phases are less intense because far less ibogaine is ingested.

If you take ibogaine for psycho-spiritual purposes, you can expect to be in bed for twelve hours. The first six hours will be extremely intense, and then you will come down from the peak as the ibogaine washes out of your body. This intense period can be pleasurable, painful, or a combination of the two. After twelve hours, you will be able to move around, eat, and talk. You will probably experience a day of mental and emotional exhaustion. After waking up from your first long sleep, you will probably feel energized and euphoric. For the next few weeks or months, you will have a lot of freedom from your emotional triggers, but this will gradually fade. Within three months, you will settle into to a baseline state. For most people, this baseline is lighter and freer than their baseline before taking ibogaine. People often find that they have resolved an issue that was causing them a lot of pain, even if this issue was not why they decided to take ibogaine. As one experienced person put it: "Ibogaine does not give you what you want, it gives you what you need."

This chapter describes the variety of experiences that people have had. The chapter is split into three sections: spiritual, emotional, and physical healing. Keep in mind that these divisions are arbitrary and in reality, the categories blend into each other.

Spiritual Healing

Many people have taken ibogaine because they felt stuck in their spiritual practice. Longtime practitioners of meditation, contemplation, or another spiritual discipline often reach a plateau. This happens because these techniques are often too soft to penetrate the fear-based mind. For many longtime practitioners, the ego has slowly claimed ownership of spirituality and twisted the practice to its own purpose.

Ibogaine can be helpful in getting unstuck. Powerful psychedelics can temporarily shatter the ego and give someone a glimpse of Being (otherwise known as God, the Tao, Nirvana, Spirit, etc). Being is confusing for many spiritual aspirants because it is not a "thing"; it is the context within which all things arise. This means that it cannot be experienced, because all experiences occur within Being. Since Being is so obvious, most spiritual practitioners overlook it because they are too busy *seeking*. Ibogaine can temporarily shatter the mind's capacity to seek, forcing you to look at what is already present. And once you truly know that freedom from ego is possible, the spiritual practice progresses much faster.

Many people have more traditional religious experiences. Instead of experiencing unity with Pure Being, they experience Being as an "other" that they communicate with. Some people label this Being as God, some label it the Spirit of Iboga, and others call it their Higher Self. Regardless of the label, people usually receive insights from this Being about their lives or humanity in general. They also receive instructions about how to live. These instructions are not perceived as rules that the person must obey, they are more like guidelines about how to avoid suffering.

Another common experience is communicating with intelligent beings that are not human. Sometimes people feel like they are communicating with beings from another planet or dimension.

Other times, people feel like they are meeting with angels or souls between lives. People who have this type of experience usually stop fearing death, because they know that something exists beyond this life. They also become less preoccupied with living up to society's ridiculous expectations.

Emotional Healing

Less people take ibogaine for emotional difficulties than for spiritual purposes or addiction interruption. This is a shame, an ibogaine session is like a decade of psychotherapy rolled into one night. Traditional therapy mainly helps people acquire intellectual insight into their emotional problems. Most people find that this mental understanding helps them make sense of their issues, but it does not lead to a real change in behavior. After years of therapy, many people continue to play out dysfunctional patterns despite wanting to change because the subconscious is far more powerful than the conscious mind.

Psychedelics like ibogaine help people go deeply into their psyche and deal with repressed pain and trauma. People often report going into their deepest fears, confronting these fears, and gaining real freedom. Ibogaine has helped many people deal with depression, anxiety, addiction to shopping, sex, and food, and many other problems.

Ibogaine's effectiveness in emotional therapy is related to its spiritual power. By taking people deeper into Being, ibogaine allows them to confront their demons. This happens because nothing can harm Being itself, and frightening thoughts and emotions lose their power when a person is more identified with Being. This explains why many people report having visions of terrible things on ibogaine while simultaneously feeling peaceful and calm.

Ibogaine has helped many people overcome depression. An excellent, insightful psychiatrist, James Gordon, wrote in his book *Unstuck* that, "Depression is not a disease...It is a sign that our lives are out of balance. It is a wake-up call." People take ibogaine for depression when they know that something is wrong but they cannot resolve the conflict in their normal state of consciousness. For many depressed people, the rational mind develops defenses against looking at the reality of their life. As long as these defenses are up, healing cannot happen. Ibogaine shocks the mind and weakens those defenses. This allows depressed people to see how their life is out of balance and gives them time to make corrections before the fearful mind can resurrect the barriers.

Ibogaine has also helped many people with post-traumatic stress disorder (PTSD). One of my friends, a former Army medic, had PSTD from the first Gulf War after witnessing what American missiles do to Iraqi children. For the next two decades, he struggled with depression, nightmares, uncontrolled rage, and alcoholism. None of the therapies he tried helped; even quitting drinking led to only marginal improvement. In 2012, he decided to take ibogaine after knowing about it for years. Right after his session, his symptoms vanished. He felt calm and happy, his mind was clear and organized, and he slept through the night for the first time in years. As the months passed, some of his symptoms returned in a much weaker form. He expressed his condition to me this way, "I can get angry but not rageful. I can get sad but not slip into chronic depression, and I can do things I was never able to do before due to my triggers being virtually nonexistent."

As with addiction interruption, ibogaine should not be viewed as a "magic bullet" for serious psychological problems. Ibogaine can help a lot, especially in the short run, but it works best when combined with other therapies. The crucial element, as always, is the clarity of the person's intentions.

Physical Healing

There are scattered reports that ibogaine has helped people with almost every physical ailment you can think of, but there is not a lot of hard data. Beyond reports from providers in the West, many people in Gabon take iboga for all manner of physical problems, especially infertility. I think this provides evidence that ibogaine helps, although we cannot know how much.

There is a lot of good evidence that ibogaine helps with chronic pain and fibromyalgia. Many people with chronic pain report an absence or major reduction in pain after a treatment, even when they took ibogaine for another issue. This has been reported by so many patients and providers that there must be truth to it. Unfortunately, no one has systematically followed up with these people, so it cannot be determined how long the effects last. It is possible that chronic pain can return after months or years.

It is also possible that ibogaine only helps with certain types of pain. For example, I interviewed two women who had chronic pain after a car accident. One reported a significant reduction in pain for up to a year after her session. The other person said that her physical pain did not lessen, but her emotional capacity to accept the pain increased, making her life much better.

There is one report of ibogaine helping a woman with severe multiple sclerosis (MS). Before her session, her MS was so advanced that she could barely swallow water, she could not feel her feet, she needed a catheter to urinate, and sometimes she could barely walk. After her session, which she took for opiate addiction, she discovered that her symptoms were in total remission. When she returned home, her doctor gave her a magnetic resonance imaging scan (MRI) and found a major reduction in the inflammation of her MS-related lesions. Around a year later, she noticed her symptoms returning, so she took a small dose of ibogaine, which eliminated her symptoms for more than a year. She took another small dose, and her symptoms did not return for eighteen months. She has not had a major MS attack since her first ibogaine session, and she has not needed conventional steroid medicines. However, she may need to take small ibogaine doses annually for the rest of her life.

Her story suggests that ibogaine offers a treatment for MS, but her experience should not be treated as proof that ibogaine can "cure" MS. It is possible that her case is special and that other MS sufferers will gain nothing. If you are interested in trying ibogaine for MS, keep in mind that this woman went off all her MS medications before taking ibogaine. This took her about five months and was not easy. Go down this path only if you are committed and you accept the possibility that your treatment may not work.

Hopefully, more research will be done on ibogaine's potential for healing pain in coming years. But since most providers are not set up to collect data, it may be a long time before it is known how effective ibogaine is for MS and other physical ailments.

CHAPTER SIX
THE LAW

This chapter is broken into two sections. The first section covers the legal status of ibogaine around the world. The second section discusses drug policies around the world and the most likely future for ibogaine.

The Legal Status of Ibogaine

Ibogaine is formally legal in one country, New Zealand. Its legalization there is a remarkable example of sanity and reason. In the early 2000s, a woman in New Zealand began providing treatments after ibogaine helped her get clean from painkillers. She collaborated with a doctor to maximize safety. In 2009, the government agency tasked with regulating drugs held a hearing on ibogaine. It noted that ibogaine assisted with opiate, methamphetamine, nicotine, and alcohol addiction, and it had a low chance of being abused. Based on this evidence, it ruled that ibogaine should be classified as a prescription medication.

Since then, no other country has followed New Zealand's example. A doctor in Brazil, Bruno Rasmussen, has been working with his government to legalize ibogaine. He believes that the government will ultimately classify it as a prescription drug, but the process may take several more years. In the meantime, ibogaine can legally be imported and used in treatments. The only restrictions are that it cannot be resold in Brazil and providers cannot advertise their services.

Ibogaine is illegal in Belgium, Denmark, France, Switzerland, Sweden, and the United States. The Belgium government allegedly banned it decades ago because a Belgian pharmaceutical company was making an ibogaine derivative and wanted to remove the competition. Denmark illegalized ibogaine after a schizophrenic woman killed herself several days after a session. The French government banned it after a man self-administered iboga and overdosed. The Swiss government made it illegal after a Swiss woman died during an ibogaine treatment in the Netherlands. I do not know why it is illegal in Sweden, although the country has the strictest drug laws in Europe.

In the United States, ibogaine was made illegal by the 1970 Controlled Substances Act. The Act made ibogaine a Schedule I substance, which means that it was considered to have a high potential for abuse, had no currently accepted medical use, and was unsafe for use under medical supervision. Ibogaine was classified this way because the government classified almost every known drug as Schedule I in 1970 and Congress has done nothing since to reexamine the law.

Despite this prohibition, ibogaine may actually become legal in the next few years by being recognized as a religious sacrament. The United States, which has the least tolerant drug policies in the Western world, ironically accepts drug use for religious purposes. In 1994, Congress legalized peyote use by Native Americans. In 2006, the US Supreme Court unanimously ruled that the Santo Daimyo cult could import and use ayahuasca, the world's second-most powerful psychedelic. In early 2013, several iboga providers who practiced Bwiti were on trial in Oregon for using ibogaine to help an addict and the judge ruled that their activities should be considered religious and therefore permissible. This single court case did nothing to change the law, but it suggests the possibility of eventual legalization.

Excluding the countries mentioned, ibogaine is unregulated everywhere else in the world. Although a lack of regulation does not technically mean that ibogaine is legal, in practice people can do what they want. Most treatment centers are in countries where its use is unregulated and clinics rarely encounter legal problems.

The Future of Ibogaine

Ibogaine will become widely used only when it has strong institutional support behind it and that requires government acceptance. I believe that ibogaine will never be accepted by governments because of its psychoactive properties, but I think that governments will readily accept an ibogaine synthetic, 18-MC, that is not psychedelic.

Governments approach drug use from two perspectives: as a medical problem and as a criminal problem. Some countries, like the United States and Sweden, focus heavily on criminalizing drugs and do almost nothing to help addicts medically. At the other end of the spectrum, Portugal has completely decriminalized drug use, even for heroin and cocaine, and treats addiction as a purely medical problem. Most countries blend the approaches: criminalizing some drug use and treating other types of use as a medical issue.

Although the approaches differ in their application, they have the same goal: the elimination of drug use in society. It is important to keep this in mind when comparing countries. For example, many people believe that the Netherlands has an enlightened attitude toward drug use because marijuana and mild psychedelics are sold in special shops. This is inaccurate. Most Dutch people frown on drug use, but they consider legalization less harmful than criminalization. This explains why, since 2001, the Dutch government has enacted more repressive criminal penalties for some drugs while simultaneously initiating heroin prescription trials and supporting medical marijuana research.

The same point applies to Portugal. In the 1990s, the country experienced an increase in drug use despite severe criminal penalties. In 1998, the government created a special commission to study the problem. The commission concluded that Portugal's policies were a total failure and recommended reversing direction. Amazingly, the government listened. It decriminalized personal possession and use of all drugs and it invested heavily in medical treatments for addicts (but kept strong punishments for dealers). In the years since, Portugal's policies have been universally recognized as successful. The country has less drug-related deaths, its HIV rate has dropped, more people are in treatment, and the overall rate of drug use is lower than in the rest of Europe.

Portugal represents a paradigm shift in international drug policy. Over the last decade, the medical approach to drug use has gained significant ground over the criminalization approach. Many countries have decriminalized possession of small amounts of drugs, and several US states have decriminalized marijuana. Five hundred economists, including several Nobel laureates, signed an open letter to the US government advocating legalization of marijuana. The world's most widely read news journal, *The Economist*, consistently advocates decriminalization. Most prominently, the Global Commission on Drug Policy called for an end to the criminal approach to drug use. This commission included seven former leaders of countries, Ronald Reagan's secretary of state, a former secretary general of the United Nations, and the former chairman of the US Federal Reserve. The commission's report stated that the "war on drugs" failed dismally all around the world and pointed out the success of public health approaches.

All of this suggests that public policy toward drugs will switch in the coming decades, but it does not imply that ibogaine will get recognition from governments. Keep in mind that the success of the medical approach is measured by its ability to reduce drug use and the harmful effects on society. No government, including Portugal's, is open to the possibility that occasionally taking drugs might be good for you.

Ibogaine is too powerful of a psychedelic for governments to be ever accept. Understand that modern society basically accepts two states of consciousness. One is an alert, focused, problem-solving state. Our educational system spends over a decade teaching us to induce and maintain this state, while coffee and nicotine help to intensify it. Society also tolerates the blankness of drinking alcohol and watching television as a necessary release valve for the pressure of remaining alert all day.

Ibogaine and other psychedelics undermine society's pressure to vacillate between these two states. Psychedelics cause people to question their conditioning and they make it easier to access a state of peaceful happiness. After taking psychedelics, people are usually less willing to spend their life swinging between states of tense vigilance and numbness. As such, psychedelics threaten the psychological foundations of modernity and can never be supported by governments.

Ibogaine would only be accepted by governments if its psychoactive properties could be removed, and one synthetic is thought to do that. Known as 18-MC, this synthetic has a molecular structure that is almost identical to ibogaine and has been shown to reduce drug use in rodents. So far, 18-MC has been administered only to rats and mice, so its effects on humans are unknown. Researchers believe that 18-MC will eliminate drug cravings without any psychedelics effects. It may also be safer for people with heart problems. 18-MC has another "advantage" over ibogaine in that it is manmade rather than naturally occurring. This means that, unlike ibogaine, it can be patented and so pharmaceutical companies can make a lot of money with it. This is important because it costs around $300 million to get the FDA to legalize a drug for prescription purposes and only large pharmaceuticals can afford these costs.

CHAPTER SEVEN
THE SCIENCE

Scientists are a long way from understanding ibogaine, but a few key lessons have been learned. First, ibogaine bonds with many of the same receptors as opiates, cocaine, alcohol, and nicotine. Ibogaine's effect on these receptors explains why people do not experience withdrawal. Second, ibogaine probably "resets" the brain to its pre-addiction state or at least moves it closer to its pre-addiction state. Third, ibogaine may induce a dream state in which unlearning old connections and learning new behaviors are accelerated. Fourth, ibogaine is toxic only in quantities that far exceed a normal dose. This chapter will summarize the research that supports these conclusions by looking at animal experiments, the effects of ibogaine on brain receptors and brainwaves, and toxicity studies.

Animal Experiments

Numerous studies with animals have proven that ibogaine reduces cravings for heroin, morphine, cocaine, alcohol, and nicotine. In these studies, researchers got mice, rats, and monkeys addicted to one of these drugs. The researchers allowed the animals to self-administer the drug through a lever in their cage and recorded how frequently they self-administered. The researchers treated the animals with ibogaine and recorded how frequently the animals self-administered the drugs after the session. They found that a single dose of ibogaine was extremely effective at eliminating self-administration of morphine, heroin, alcohol, and nicotine. For cocaine, the most effective treatment involved giving the animal one dose of ibogaine per week for three weeks. This suggested that crack and cocaine addiction required a longer treatment protocol.

The other interesting finding from these studies was that lower drug self-administration was maintained long after the ibogaine had washed out of the animal's system. This suggested that ibogaine was resetting the brain to a pre-addictive state. This conclusion was supported by a few other studies. In one, rats were given ibogaine before receiving cocaine; as a result, the rats did not become sensitized to cocaine. In another, mice that were given ibogaine after receiving morphine did not develop a tolerance to morphine. However, the conclusion that ibogaine resets the brain has not been proven; it has been inferred from other observations. Even if it is true, we do not know how completely ibogaine resets the brain. In all likelihood, the resetting is partial.

Effects on Brain Receptors

The human brain is very complicated and ibogaine effects in the brain in multiple ways, so researchers do not know exactly how ibogaine effects the brain. Here is what they do know.

After ibogaine is ingested, the body metabolizes some of it into something called noribogaine. Both ibogaine and noribogaine affect numerous receptors in the brain. Among these are the same receptors that opiates bond with. Ibogaine also seems to ease the transmission of information along opioid neurotransmitters, which effectively increasing their sensitivity; this effect may be permanent. This finding explains why ibogaine is such a powerful healing tool for opiate addiction. It bonds with the same receptors as opiates while improving the function of opioid neurotransmitters. In doing so, ibogaine prevents withdrawal while the opiates flush out of the system, and it prevents cravings from reemerging for a long time.

Ibogaine influences the receptors for two major neurotransmitters, serotonin and dopamine. These neurotransmitters are associated with feeling happy and confident. They are also the major point of influence in the brain for cocaine, crack, and meth. These drugs make a person feel euphoric by causing spikes in serotonin and dopamine. After extended drug use, these receptors adjust to the artificially elevated levels and become less sensitive to these neurotransmitters. These drugs also cause the brain to produce less serotonin and dopamine. This explains why heavy drug users develop a tolerance and eventually cannot feel happy at all without taking drugs.

Several studies with animals have shown that ibogaine increases the amount of serotonin that the brain releases, and blocks the brain from reabsorbing excess serotonin. Taken together, these effects increase the amount of serotonin available in the brain. Ibogaine does not increase the amount of dopamine released, but it decreases how quickly dopamine receptors expel dopamine. This means that the dopamine receptors fire more frequently and therefore there is more dopamine in the brain.

These findings explain why ibogaine provides short-term relief from cocaine addiction. The brain of a cocaine user requires high levels of serotonin and dopamine to feel normal, and ibogaine increases those neurotransmitters. Ibogaine must also reset the neurotransmitters; otherwise, the addiction would return full-force within a few days. Based on evidence reported by providers, cocaine addiction returns after a few days, but it is weakened. With people who take multiple treatments over several weeks, cravings can be almost eliminated. The most likely explanation for this permanent reduction in cravings is that the receptors have been reset to a pre-addiction state.

Ibogaine is known to affect three other receptors, but the consequences of these effects remain mysterious because the receptors are poorly understood. Some studies have found that ibogaine's strongest effect is on N-methyl-D-aspartate (NMDA) receptors. Researchers know that NMDA is associated with altered states of consciousness, but they know little else, and so they cannot specify what effect ibogaine is having. Ibogaine also bonds with a class of receptors called sigma receptors. Scientists have found that activating these receptors makes people feel happy, but otherwise they know very little about sigma receptors. Finally, many studies have found that ibogaine blocks certain nicotinic receptors, but again, it is not clear what this means.

Brainwaves

Another set of studies examines the effect of ibogaine on the brain's electrical activity. These studies involved measuring brainwaves of animals on ibogaine using an electroencephalogram, more commonly known as an EEG. The studies found that animals entered a state similar to the "rapid eye movement" stage of sleep, which is the stage when dreaming occurs. This parallels reports from people who have a lot of experience with psychedelics. They claim that ibogaine induces a dream state that is different from the hallucinations induced by psychedelics like LSD.

Ibogaine's effect on the brain can be understood through its ability to induce a dream state. Dreams may be a way for the brain to process experiences, make new connections, and learn new behaviors. An addiction can be viewed as a maladaptive learned behavior where the brain connects drug use with being rewarded. Ibogaine brings a person into the dream state while still awake. Once in the dream state, the person can consciously unlearn harmful behaviors and learn positive behaviors more quickly than in a normal, waking state. But again, the evidence on this matter is far from conclusive.

Toxicity Studies

It is widely known among Bwiti practitioners and ibogaine providers that high doses of ibogaine can be fatal. Fortunately, a hazardous dose far exceeds the amount given in an ibogaine session. In a normal addiction-interruption session, the quantity of ibogaine in a person's body will almost never exceed 30 mg/kg ("mg/kg" is the standard measurement for an ibogaine dose; it stands for milligrams of ibogaine per kilograms of body weight).

In studies with animals, researchers found that the median fatal dose was 145 mg/kg for rats and 175 mg/kg for mice. Mice that received 100 mg/kg had no adverse reactions, but rats had some neural toxicity. In another study, researchers gave some monkeys an oral dose of 25 mg/kg and injected others with 100 mg/kg. None of the monkeys were found to have negative health effects.

There is only one reported case of a fatal ibogaine overdose in the West. The person acquired the iboga root bark himself and ate it without knowing anything about the plant. It is not known how much he took, but when he died fifty-three hours after ingesting it, his blood still had high concentrations of ibogaine. Considering that ibogaine has a half-life of 7.5 hours, it could safely be assumed that he hit 200 mg/kg at the peak of his session. His example should serve as a warning that ibogaine should be taken under the supervision of a knowledgeable provider.

CHAPTER EIGHT
THREE CURRENT ISSUES

This chapter covers three growing problems in the ibogaine world. The first problem is the recent proliferation of providers. The second is that the demand for iboga may outstrip supply in the coming years, leading to shortages or total unavailability. The third is the tendency to fetishize ibogaine by treating is a miracle and solution to all of life's problems.

The proliferation of new ibogaine providers is not a problem in itself. The more ibogaine providers there are, the more people can be helped. However, some newer providers are inexperienced and still recovering from their own addictions. Providing ibogaine requires a good deal of training and a high degree of emotional stability. Someone who just detoxed from heroin is not qualified on either count. Even worse, a small number of providers are motivated by a desire to make money or feed their egos. They are threatened by other ibogaine providers and treat them as rivals. Some have even tried to frighten potential clients away from their competitors by claiming that their competitors are unsafe. These providers undermine the general culture of cooperation among providers and they selfishly alarm people who come to them seeking help.

If you are looking for a provider, find one who has been in business for a few years or has spent at least one year training with a more established provider. Find a provider with a lot of good references. Do not be put off by a few bad online reviews (no one can please everyone), but avoid providers who consistently leave their clients dissatisfied. Do not trust a provider who eagerly tells you scary stories about the competition. In all likelihood, he is trying to capture your business for himself. The best ibogaine providers put your needs first, and most will gladly help you find the treatment center that best suits your needs.

The second problem in the ibogaine world is supply. Right now, all ibogaine comes from the iboga bushes in Gabon and Cameroon. Because ibogaine is found only in the root, these bushes do not need to be destroyed; a quarter of the root structure can be harvested each year, and the plant can be left alive. Unfortunately, many harvesters are uprooting the entire bush and diminishing the overall supply of iboga.

Around 2000, the demand for ibogaine rapidly increased. Within a few years, providers experienced shortages in their supply chains. Some enterprising people in Gabon responded by planting more bushes and harvesting only the root structure, but their efforts have not kept pace with the accelerating demand. No one knows exactly how long the existing supply of bushes will last, but people in Gabon predict that there will be serious shortages in five to ten years. If this happens, the best-case scenario is that ibogaine will be widely unavailable for eight years. A shortage will force people in Gabon and the Western Hemisphere to begin planting their own iboga bushes (the climate in Central and South America is appropriate). The plant takes at least eight years to mature, so ibogaine will be unavailable for that time. In the worst case, ibogaine will never be available again in large quantities.

Another source of ibogaine is the voacanga tree. This tree grows in many countries in West Central Africa and reportedly grows in India. The voacanga contains small quantities of ibogaine. But because no one currently harvests it on a large scale, there is no way to know if these trees can replace iboga bushes as the world's main source of ibogaine.

The third problem is an unwarranted fetishizing of ibogaine. This is a common reaction in people who have had amazing ibogaine sessions and it leads to a number of mental traps. People who are radically transformed during a session may decide that ibogaine *alone* is responsible for their new condition. This ultimately robs them of their inherent power and causes them to neglect other psychological and spiritual practices. They may also believe that ibogaine can solve all their problems and they become lazy in dealing with their other issues. Many people also take the insights they have on ibogaine as absolute, revealed truth. This posture makes them very close-minded because they believe that no one is as enlightened as they are.

This fetishizing is not only harmful for the individual, it is harmful for the whole ibogaine movement. Evangelists for ibogaine, despite being sincere, often end up making promises that ibogaine cannot deliver on. People hear these promises, go for an ibogaine session, and end up disappointed because they expected a miracle.

If you are considering an ibogaine session, please take any wild promises with a grain of salt. Ibogaine is an incredible gift, but it is not a magic bullet. It is a tool that will give you an amazing start on a new chapter of your life, but how you actually live this next chapter is up to you. The final chapter of this book will help you decide whether or not ibogaine is right for you.

CHAPTER NINE

IS IBOGAINE RIGHT FOR ME?

If you are considering whether or not to take ibogaine, ask yourself this question: *Is my desire to change greater than my fear of the unknown?*

If your honest answer is no, ibogaine cannot help you. In a very real sense, ibogaine does not add anything new. It merely works with the elements already present in your consciousness. If you take ibogaine and cling in terror to your illusions and addictions, ibogaine will respect your choice and not overwhelm you. You will have an unpleasant experience and ultimately learn nothing.

This has happened many times, almost always with people who acquire ibogaine without any sacrifice (for example, people who are wealthy or have family members drag them to a clinic). I believe that this is the cause of ibogaine's high success rate. Ibogaine sessions are fairly expensive and usually require travelling to a third world country. These high barriers weed out almost everyone who is not truly committed. If ibogaine were easily available, it would probably have a lower success rate.

If you bought this book because you are trying to help save a friend or family member, this may be difficult to read. You may hope that ibogaine can force your loved one to stop hurting herself, but it simply does not have that power. People are free to choose their own lives, and for some reason, many people choose to suffer. All you can do is love them and be there when they are finally ready to change.

If your answer to the question above is a tentative yes, ibogaine is perfect for you. An ibogaine session will bring you face to face with your demons and give you the resources to confront them head on. In the weeks and months that follow, your fears will be too weak to control your thinking. If you use the time wisely, your desire to be free will overcome your fears when they inevitably return. This is true whether you are an addict, a person with psychological pain, a spiritual seeker, or all of the above.

Finally, if your answer to the question above is an unambiguous yes, you probably do not need ibogaine. You have the capacity within you to be free at any moment, so stop waiting and just do it.

If you feel strongly that you should take

ibogaine, I recommend not delaying another moment. Find a reputable provider, schedule a session, and start planning a supportive environment that will help you once your session is over. And if ibogaine is not part of your path, that is just as good. Whatever you choose, I wish you all the best in finding your happiness and freedom.

NOTES

Chapter 1

- James Fernandez, *Bwiti: An Ethnography of the Religious Imagination in Africa* (Princeton, NJ: Princeton University Press, 1982).

- J. W. Fernandez and R. L. Fernandez, "Returning to the Path: The Use of Iboga in an Equatorial African Ritual Context and the Binding of Time, Space, and Social Relationships," *The Alkaloids* 56 (2001): 235–247.

Chapter 2

- The section on Howard Lotsof is mainly from Kenneth Alper, Dana Beal, and Charles D. Kaplan, "A Contemporary History of Ibogaine in the United States and Europe," *The Alkaloids* 56 (2001): 249–281.

- The section on Eric Taub comes from personal interviews with him.

- The section on Dimitri Mugianis comes from an interview I conducted with him in 2012 for *Iboradio*, an online radio show, as well as personal conversations.

Chapter 3

- This section aggregates about a dozen interviews that I conducted with providers in 2012. Several experienced providers read the chapter and approved its contents.

- This was the study on fatalities. See Kenneth Alper, Marina Stajic, and James Gill, "Fatalities Temporally Associated with the Ingestion of Ibogaine," *Journal of Forensic Sciences* 57 (2012).

Chapter 4

- This section is based on discussions with many providers and people who have taken ibogaine.

- James Gordon Smith, *Unstuck* (New York, NY: Penguin Press, 2008).

- Damon Matthew Smith, "Ibogaine and PTSD: The Quieted Rage," http://ibogaine-treatment.org/?p=51.

- The woman I interviewed about MS asked to remain anonymous.

Chapter 5

- For a review of the science, see Kenneth Alper, "Ibogaine: A Review," *The Alkaloids* 56 (2001): 1–34.

Chapter 6

- The New Zealand government's ruling can be found at http://www.medsafe.govt.nz/profs/class/mccmin03nov2009.htm.

- Caroline Chatwin, *Drug Policy Harmonization and the European Union* (Palgrave Macmillan, 2011), compares drug policies around the world.

- For information about 18-MC, see Hamilton Keegan, "Ibogaine: Can It Cure Addiction without the Hallucinogenic Trip?" *Village Voice* (2010).

Chapter 7

- This discussion is based on my personal experience and conversations with providers.

MEDICAL DISCLAIMER

This book is NOT a substitute for working with an experienced provider. Do not take ibogaine by yourself – you will have a better experience and better outcomes if you work with an expert.

Although the author has made every effort to ensure that the information in this book was correct at press time, the author does not assume and hereby disclaim any liability to any party for any loss, damage, or disruption caused by errors or omissions, whether such errors or omissions result from negligence, accident, or any other cause.

This book is not intended as a substitute for the medical advice of physicians. The reader should regularly consult a physician in matters relating to his/her health and particularly with respect to any symptoms that may require diagnosis or medical attention.

CONTACT AUTHORS

The authors can be contacted in the following ways:
Email: ibeginagain@aol.com
Phone: 646-225-6622 (this is a US number)
Website: www.erictaub.info

Made in the USA
Las Vegas, NV
19 June 2021